+   +

THE HEART OF GOD'S
STORY

Know His Face. Thrive in His Space.
Extend His Grace.

+

GEORGE H. GUTHRIE

LifeWay Press®
Nashville, Tennessee

Published by LifeWay Press® • © 2016 George H. Guthrie

ISBN 978-1-4300-5516-7 • Item 006104046

Dewey decimal classification: 220.95
Subject headings: BIBLE / BIBLE—HISTORY / REVELATION /
PROVIDENCE AND GOVERNMENT OF GOD

To order additional copies of this resource, write to LifeWay Resources Customer Service; One LifeWay Plaza; Nashville, TN 37234-0113; phone toll free 800.458.2772; order online at *www.lifeway.com*; email *orderentry@lifeway.com*; fax 615.251.5933; or visit the LifeWay Christian Store serving you.

Printed in the United States of America

Groups Ministry Publishing • LifeWay Resources
One LifeWay Plaza • Nashville, TN 37234-0152

CONTENTS

The Author

Dr. George H. Guthrie serves as the Benjamin W. Perry Professor of Bible at Union University in Jackson, Tennessee. He is the author of numerous articles and has written a dozen books, including *2 Corinthians in Baker Exegetical Commentary on the New Testament* series, *The NIV Application Commentary: Hebrews*, and the Hebrews section of *Commentary on the New Testament Use of the Old Testament*.

As the architect of the Read the Bible for Life biblical-literacy initiative, Guthrie has written or edited five tools, including this Bible study (LifeWay, 2016), *Read the Bible for Life Bible study* (LifeWay, 2010), *Read the Bible for Life: Your Guide to Understanding and Living God's Word* (B&H, 2011), *A Reader's Guide to the Bible* (LifeWay, 2011), and *Reading God's Story: A Chronological Daily Bible* (B&H, 2011). Guthrie has participated in translation projects, such as the revision of the New Living Translation, and has served as a consultant on the Holman Christian Standard Bible, the New Century Version, and the English Standard Version.

Guthrie holds PhD and MDiv degrees from Southwestern Baptist Theological Seminary and a ThM from Trinity Evangelical Divinity School. At Union University he led in the establishment of and serves as Senior Fellow in the Ryan Center for Biblical Studies, which is committed to promoting sound Bible reading, study, and interpretation in local churches.

Dr. Guthrie has been married to the incomparable Pat Guthrie for more than a quarter of a century, and they have two grown children, Joshua and Anna. Dr. and Mrs. Guthrie attend Northbrook Church, which they helped plant more than 20 years ago.

Introduction

Welcome to *The Heart of God's Story*. Think of this Bible study's title from two vantage points.

1. In this study we'll identify central themes (the heart) that shape the story of Scripture from the beginning to the end. We'll focus especially on—
   - the intersection of God's face—the emphasis on God's presence as a key to the biblical narrative;
   - God's space—the fact that God always creates places for people to walk with and know Him;
   - the extension of God's grace in the world.

2. *The Heart of God's Story* also points us to God's heart—His desire or passion—revealed in the story of Scripture. As we learn to read and study Scripture in greater depth, we rightly engage our minds in fresh ways. In fact, we're to love God with our mind, as Jesus Himself reminds us in Mark 12:29-30. But those verses also say we're to love God with all our heart, soul, and strength. In other words, God wants us to love Him with all we are, investing our whole lives in a relationship with Him. Working out such a meaningful, intimate, life-grounding relationship constitutes the beat of God's heart, which becomes the purpose of our lives and the driving force behind God's mission revealed in Scripture.

As we work our way through this study, we'll unpack these central, life-orienting topics in a way that has the potential to change us forever. God's Word, after all, doesn't come back to Him empty (see Isa. 55:11). But to see life-changing results, we'll need to engage with this Bible study in ways that will open our lives to the work of the Spirit of God.

How to Use This Bible Study

This Bible study is divided into six weeks of study with both group-study and personal-study components.

Weekly Group Sessions

Each week begins with suggestions for a small-group session, divided into three sections.

1. "Start: Sharing Your Heart" presents questions that can be used to open the small-group discussion. In week 1 these questions help members get to know one another and prepare members to watch the first video. In weeks 2–6 these opening discussion questions provide a review of the video from the previous group session and enable members to process their personal study since the previous group session. This introductory discussion time will work most effectively when members of the group have completed the personal study for the week. If you're completing this study alone, consider talking through the discussion questions with a friend and sharing your insights on what you're learning.

2. "Watch: Hearing God's Heart" provides key statements from the video to be shown during the session, along with lines for taking notes.

3. "Discuss: Responding to God's Heart" suggests questions for discussing the video session the group has watched. Group members will be encouraged to discern the truths of God's Word, to connect the teachings of God's Word in meaningful ways, and to engage personally with the story of Scripture.

Weekly Personal Study

Each week's personal study is divided into three parts.

1. "Meeting God in the Story: Rhythms of the Heart" is for everyone. Whether or not you record answers to all the questions, they'll stimulate your thinking about the passages of Scripture you're reading each day.

2. "Going Deeper: Depths of the Heart" is optional. It's provided for participants who have the time and energy to dig deeper into the Word each week. Specifically, this section will teach you the basics of inductive Bible study.

   Inductive Bible study is an approach to Bible study that explores what the original author intended to communicate through writing and its significance for us today. In this approach to Bible study, we'll consider issues of context, word meanings, the type of literature, important theological concepts, and ways to apply the text appropriately.

3. "Journaling: Expressions of the Heart" provides pages at the end of each week's personal study and at the back of this book for you to use in whatever way you find helpful. If you run out of space in the space under a daily reading, allow your notes to overflow here. This is also a good place to record key insights from the week's personal study or questions you want to ask in the next small-group session.

Online Tools

Tools designed to equip you for more effective Bible reading and study are provided at *LifeWay.com/HeartofGodsStory*. There you will find video interviews on how to understand various portions of the Bible, overviews of theological contexts, instructions for completing word studies, and a template for Bible study.

Call to a Joyful Commitment

If God's Word and God's ways are to have a great impact on our lives, we'll have to be open to God's instruction and committed to making space in our lives for God to work. Thankfully, such a commitment is a joy, not a burden. Think of the excitement you feel when you spend focused time with your spouse or a close friend. Setting aside space for a date or a dinner, rather than being burdensome, brings renewal in the midst of very busy, sometimes draining lives.

Here are some ways you can work with your facilitator, your group, and the Holy Spirit as you complete this study.

1. Make a commitment now to attend every group session. Because *The Heart of God's Story* deals with the central themes of the Bible and thus the very purpose of our lives, we need to devote time to think through those themes and their implications.

2. Plan ahead to make specific time each day to complete "Rhythms of the Heart: Meeting God in the Story" in each week's personal study. Life space (the actual minutes in our day) and heart space (the emotional and spiritual attention we give God and/or other people or things) are precious commodities in life. We have to make a conscious decision to commit both to build our relationship with the Lord. A great place to begin is simply to set aside a predetermined time and place to meet with God each day. Where and when will you have your time with the Lord to complete the reading and learning activities in this study?

3. Enlist an encouragement partner. Ecclesiastes 4:9 says, "Two are better than one because they have a good reward for their efforts." Plan to pray for your partner each day and perhaps to meet with your partner once a week. Share with each other the things the Lord is teaching you. Encourage each other to stick with the study to the end.

4. We're all at various places in our relationships with the Lord. Feel free to live at the level where God has you at present. If you decide to complete only "Rhythms of the Heart" in your personal study each week, that's great. But aim to complete those daily readings with depth of thought and prayer. If you want to dig deeper by completing "Depths of the Heart" inductive Bible study, that's also great. Enjoy the process of learning. Maybe some weeks you won't have time to complete all the personal study. That's OK. If you struggle a bit one week, go ahead and attend the group session and learn from the group. We can all support and learn from one another.

5. At the same time, stretch yourself to grow in your reading and study of God's good Word. Reading the personal study each week is good, but you'll grow a lot more by completing the suggested activities. As you consistently spend time in the Word, your spiritual muscles will get stronger. As that happens during this study, feel free to dip into "Depths of the Heart," even if you take only very small steps. Do this for joy, not under compulsion, but don't rule out your ability to learn at the higher levels of the study.

6. Apply what you're learning. *The Heart of God's Story* emphasizes that mere head knowledge isn't the endgame for Bible reading and study. God is after nothing less than the transformation of your life. Therefore, you need to apply what you learn in Bible study. Each week seek to put something you learn into action. The suggested learning activities will help you live out this commitment.

7. Pray every day for yourself and the others in your group. Engaging with God's good Word is a spiritual dynamic, so spiritual forces are at work as you seek to grow in Bible reading and study. Therefore, you and your group need to pray for one another. Prayer will really make a difference in your group's understanding and application of God's Word.

Welcome to the study. Let's have a great time exploring *The Heart of God's Story*.

WEEK 1

You Are Made for God's Story

START

SHARING YOUR HEART

Introduce yourself. Ask everyone to share what they hope to gain from this study.

**Take a moment to answer the following questions.
Then discuss your answers as a group.**

1. Apart from the Bible, what's your favorite story and why?

2. What makes a story great?

3. What are keys to understanding the heart or main point of any story?

4. Why do you think so much of the Bible is in story form?

5. How are the stories of the Bible the same as and different from your favorite stories?

6. How can we read Bible stories in ways that will change us?

Study with your group.

- In this group session you'll watch video session 1. As you watch, complete the viewer guide on the next page.
- During the following week each person should complete the personal studies in week 1 of this workbook. These lessons will expand on the video teaching you've watched.
- In group session 2 you'll discuss the material you've studied during week 1. Then you'll watch video session 2 before completing week 2 in this Bible study book during the following week. Each subsequent group session follows this pattern.
- At the end of the six weeks, an optional session is provided on page 134 for groups that want to review personal notes, ask questions, or share journal entries from *The Heart of God's Story*.

WATCH

HEARING GOD'S HEART
What Makes a Great Story?

1. _____

2. Vivid _____

3. Great _____

4. _____

5. Big _____

6. Familiarity or _____

7. Connection to _____

8. A powerful _____

Our Love of Stories Is Not an Accident

Stories are at the heart of what God is up to in the _____.

Stories affect our _____ in a way that other forms of communication do not.

God has given us much of His _____ in the form of stories.

We can't understand the _____ in its beauty and its fullness if we don't understand the whole of the story.

Why God Has Made Us Story People

1. To _____ us into the story

2. To _____ us by the story

3. To _____ us for the story

Purposes of the Lord's Supper

1. To _____ this part of the story

2. To _____ the story to others

PERSONAL NOTES

....

....

....

....

Video sessions available for purchase at *LifeWay.com/HeartofGodsStory*
or for streaming with a subscription to *smallgroup.com*

DISCUSS

RESPONDING TO GOD'S HEART

1. What's one main point that arrested your attention in the video session? How could that insight make a difference in your life?

2. Robert McKee has written, "Storytelling is the most powerful way to put ideas into the world today."[1] Do you agree? Can you think of an example?

3. The research Dr. Guthrie shared about the brain is interesting. What are the various ways stories move us? Is being moved by a story always a good thing?

4. What are some ways we can grow in having a grasp on the story of Scripture as a whole?

1. Robert McKee, as quoted in Shahnaz Bahman and Helen Maffini, *Developing Children's Emotional Intelligence* (New York: Continuum International, 2008), 56.

MEETING GOD IN THE STORY

RHYTHMS OF THE HEART

DAY 1 • *GENESIS 37*

This week we'll begin our journey by reading one of the great stories in Scripture, which forms a very special hinge in the grand story of the Bible. Its importance is seen in the amount of space given to it in Genesis, the Bible's book of beginnings. The story picks up as the sons of Jacob (named Israel, for whom the nation is named) were having a squabble, and the story focuses on Joseph, who was destined to have a very important role in the history of his family.

How does the story draw you in?

What's your first impression of Joseph?

What do you learn about Joseph from the author?

What are key turning points in the story?

A video interview that explains how to understand story literature in the Old Testament can be found at *LifeWay.com/HeartofGodsStory.*

DAY 2 • *GENESIS 39*

The scene shifts to Egypt, where Joseph was sold to Pharaoh's captain of the guard, Potiphar. You may have noticed that a key phrase is repeated several times (hint: it has to do with "the Lord"). Underline that phrase. This is the heart of the chapter.

In what ways was God working behind the scenes as the hero of this story?

Stories in the Bible often move ahead on the basis of a crisis. What was the crisis here, and what was its outcome?

How did Joseph respond to the crisis? How was he being shaped to be used in the grander story?

What crisis in your life needs perspective today?

DAY 3 • *GENESIS 40:1–41:45*

Dreams are significant in biblical culture, and this theme is prominent in this part of Joseph's story.

In what way are we drawn in to the story within a story in chapter 40?

Did you pick up on the play on words in 40:20?

What are the two meanings of "lifted up the heads"?

How does the time frame shift in chapter 41?

How did God use Joseph to extend grace in the world?

How can you extend God's blessing to someone around you today?

DAY 4 • *GENESIS 41:46–42:38*

As the story develops, Joseph has been moved to a place of power and authority, while his family in the land of Canaan has been forced to action by the famine. The story is tension-filled, especially in relation to the way Joseph dealt with his brothers.

What are the satisfying elements of the story at this point?

Why do you think Joseph waited to reveal himself? You may see hints in the narrative. (Think, *Where was the rest of the family, including his younger brother?*)

What act of kindness—the extending of grace—in chapter 42 caused a crisis?

How does Joseph's story thus far illustrate this quotation?

Stories have power. They delight, enchant, touch, teach, recall, inspire, motivate, and challenge. They help us understand. They imprint a picture on our minds. Want to make a point or raise an issue? Tell a story.[1]
JANET LITHERLAND

Is there a crisis in your life at present that might actually be a way God is working in your life?

DAY 5 • *GENESIS 43–44*

Caught in a difficult situation, the brothers were forced to return to Egypt. The story moves in two directions. Joseph took the brothers to his home, inviting them closer to him (eating a meal together was a high form of hospitality). But he also created a bigger crisis for them when they left.

What was that crisis?

Why do you think Joseph did this?

Can you think of a redemptive purpose?

Are there times when grace backs us into a corner as we're confronted with our own sin?

How can God change you through this part of the story?

Praise God today that He lovingly confronts us with sin to heal us of it.

DAY 6 • GENESIS 45:1-15; 50:15-26

We now come to the climax of the story of Joseph, when he revealed his identity to his brothers.

What's deeply satisfying about this part of the story?

As the story progresses, Joseph sent for his father and the rest of the family, moving them to Egypt (our reading skips a good bit of this, but feel free to read it).

In what ways is the story of Joseph a wonderful embodiment of grace?

How does the end of the story in chapter 50 underscore the nature of God's grace?

There's an important pattern here. Can you think of someone else who was rejected by His people and became the source of their salvation and the salvation of other nations as well?

In what ways is Joseph's story an important part of our story—our history—as believers?

As we discussed in the group session, Robert McKee has written, "Storytelling is the most powerful way to put ideas into the world today."[2] What ideas do you believe God intends to put into the world through the story of Joseph?

How can God use the story of Joseph to prepare us to live God's story more effectively in the world?

Take a moment to thank God for the ways grace has been expressed in your life. Thank Him for drawing you into His story. How does God want to use you to share the story of His grace today?

SCRIPTURE MEMORY

HIDING HIS WORD IN YOUR HEART

Joseph said to them, "Don't be afraid. Am I in the place of God? You planned evil against me; God planned it for good."
GENESIS 50:19-20

1. Janet Litherland, *Storytelling from the Bible* (Colorado Springs: Meriwether, 1991), 3.
2. Robert McKee, as quoted in Shahnaz Bahman and Helen Maffini, *Developing Children's Emotional Intelligence* (New York: Continuum International, 2008), 56.

GOING DEEPER

DEPTHS OF THE HEART
Genesis 50:15-26

NOTE: Although the "Depths of the Heart" study comes at the end of the week's readings, you can complete it throughout the week alongside the daily readings in "Rhythms of the Heart" if you prefer.

This section will lead you step-by-step through an inductive study of the passage, using tools such as a study Bible, a Bible dictionary, and word-study helps. A template for Bible study can be found at *LifeWay.com/ HeartofGodsStory*.

1. **Gather your tools, beginning with a good study Bible and a Bible dictionary.**

STUDY BIBLES TO CONSIDER

Choose a study Bible that uses the primary translation you use for reading and study.

HCSB Study Bible
NIV Zondervan Study Bible
ESV Study Bible
NLT Study Bible

BIBLE DICTIONARIES TO CONSIDER

Holman Illustrated Bible Dictionary
Zondervan Illustrated Bible Dictionary
Baker Illustrated Bible Dictionary

2. **Thoughtfully read the passage in at least three different translations, noting any differences in the translations.**

A video on comparing Bible translations can
be found at *LifeWay.com/HeartofGodsStory.*

3. What's the broader literary context of the passage, both in relation to Genesis and in relation to the books that follow?

You may want to read Genesis 37–50 for context as you begin.

One way to discern the broader context of a Scripture passage is to look at an outline of the whole book, which you can find in your study Bible or Bible dictionary. Look up Genesis in one of those tools and write your insights here.

Where does this passage fit? That is, what comes before it and after it?

How does the passage function as a bridge between what comes before it and what follows it (the Book of Exodus)?

4. Read Genesis 50:15-26 again very closely, answering the following questions.

What's the setting of the passage, both in terms of time and place?

What's the nature of the relationships among the main characters?

What are the most significant actions in the passage, and what's the effect of those actions?

If you had to identify the main theme of the passage, what would it be and why, based on the text itself?

How would you divide the passage into three main movements?

5. Choose two or three words from the passage to study. Choose words that seem theologically significant, those that are repeated, or those that are found at a turning point in the story.

An overview of how to do word studies can be found at *LifeWay.com/HeartofGodsStory*.

What words have you selected for study?

What's the range of possible meanings for the Hebrew words?

Identify three to five other passages for each term in which this same Hebrew word is used in a similar way.

Based on the context of the passage, what do you think are the best translations of the words as they're used in this passage?

6. Read the notes in your study Bible.

If you also have access to commentaries, use them now.
Here are a few commentaries to consider for further study:

Mathews, Kenneth A. *Genesis 11:27–50:26. The New American Commentary.* Nashville: B&H, 2005.

Waltke, Bruce K. *Genesis: A Commentary.* Grand Rapids, MI: Zonderan, 2001.

Walton, John H. *Genesis. The NIV Application Commentary.* Grand Rapids, MI: Zondervan, 2001.

Wenham, Gordon J. *Word Biblical Commentary.* Vol. 2, *Genesis 16–50.* Grand Rapids, MI: Zondervan, 2015. (Advanced)

What are your key insights into the passage?

7. How does this passage contribute to broader theological themes in the Bible? Provide examples of cross-references to other Scripture passages.

An overview of how to study the broader theological context in the Bible can be found at *LifeWay.com/HeartofGodsStory*.

Theme 1:

Theme 2:

8. Apply the passage.

What would the passage have meant to the original readers of Genesis? What was the main point for them?

In what ways are we similar to the original audience? How are we different?

To what various aspects of our lives might the truth of this passage apply?

What's a specific application for your life?

Further insights on studying and reading Scripture more effectively can be found at *LifeWay.com/HeartofGodsStory*.

JOURNALING

EXPRESSIONS OF THE HEART

Getting to the Heart of God's Story

t way ... thes
hom ... e has a pointe ... en of
e universe. ... e is th ... radiance
ire, ... d H ... sust ins ...
ur ... atio ... for sir ... He sat down at th ...
igh ... e beca ... e h ...
herited is superior ... eirs. For to which of the angels did He ev ...
You are My Son; today ... have become Your Father," or again, "I
e His Father, and He will be My Son?" When He again brings Hi ...
orn into the world, He says: "And all God's angels must worship H ...

START

SHARING YOUR HEART

Start the session by sharing what group members learned or truths that were especially meaningful during last week's personal study. If needed, use the following review questions.

1. What's one main point that arrested your attention in the previous session's video or in the past week's personal study? How could that insight make a difference in your life?

2. Why do you think Dr. Guthrie chose the story of Joseph as a follow-up to the previous session's video? What role does this story play in the Bible's grand story? How does this story help draw us into the story of Scripture?

3. How did your understanding of Joseph's character change during the six days of reading?

4. In what ways does this story parallel the story of Jesus? How can this story help shape us to be better proclaimers of the Bible's grand story?

Study with your group.

- Pray before watching video session 2.
- As you watch, complete the viewer guide on the next page.
- Following the video, use the discussion questions provided to finish your time together as a group.
- Encourage everyone to complete the personal study for week 2 before the next group session.

WATCH

HEARING GOD'S HEART
Beauty in the Bookends of the Bible

- Genesis 1–3

- Revelation 19–22

Key Themes at the Heart
of God's Story

1. Extending God's _____

   Grace: God's trustworthy _____ and _____ extended
   to us as He gifts us with all the good things we need

2. Thriving in God's _____

   The garden foreshadows the _____ in the wilderness.

   The new Jerusalem is both a garden and a sort of tabernacle
   or _____.

3. Knowing God's _____

Made in God's Image

1. A very _____ part of creation

   Image reflects _____.

2. Our _____ with God and His walking with us

   The gospel means that where you think life stops with death is actually the place where it _____, as we die to ourselves and experience resurrection life in Jesus Christ.

PERSONAL NOTES

....
....
....
....
....
....
....
....
....
....
....

Video sessions available for purchase at *LifeWay.com/HeartofGodsStory*
or for streaming with a subscription to *smallgroup.com*

DISCUSS

RESPONDING TO GOD'S HEART

1. What's your response to the parallels between Genesis 1–3 and Revelation 19–22? Which parallel is your favorite?

2. What impact should the parallels between Genesis 1–3 and Revelation 19–22 have on our lives? Did you feel pulled into the story of Scripture by this part of the video? If so, in what ways?

3. How do you think knowing God's face—a personal relationship with God on a daily basis—is experienced in our lives?

4. Dr. Guthrie showed that both Genesis and Revelation demonstrate God's commitment to providing spaces for us to walk with Him. What's a special space in your life for meeting God? Why?

5. In the portion of the video on extending God's grace, we saw that God is very giving in all kinds of ways. Why do you think most people don't live grateful lives? How can we as a church be more effective at extending God's grace in the world?

MEETING GOD IN THE STORY

RHYTHMS OF THE HEART

DAY 1 • *GENESIS 1:1–2:4*

The first chapter of the Bible is breathtakingly beautiful. Take your time and use your imagination as you read it. Notice that rhythm and order are built into this amazing hymn reflecting on God's creation of the world. Also notice that days 4–6 of creation correspond to days 1–3. After reading the whole chapter, list what God created on each day.

Day 1:

Day 2:

Day 3:

Day 4:

Day 5:

Day 6:

In what ways is God the hero of the hymn?

What aspects of this passage speak of order and beauty?

What was good about all God created (see 1:31)?

How did the seventh day balance God's work of creation?

How does this chapter arrest your interest and draw you into the story of the Bible?

Take a moment to thank God for His creative work and for two specific things He's created that you can enjoy today.

DAY 2 • *GENESIS 2:5-25*

Genesis now zooms in on one aspect of creation, specifically the creation of human beings. We're told more about the role of human beings in a special garden (think Yosemite National Park rather than the vegetable garden in your backyard). We're also told of the creation of woman. The word *helper* (v. 18), a term often used of God Himself in the Bible, refers to someone who uniquely stands in a complementary role to meet needs in the life of the man that he can't meet for himself. The relationship was one of mutual support. God brought all kinds of animals to the man to show the man his need and to emphasize his authority over the animals as he named them. But the climax came when woman was made from man, and verse 23 is an exuberant "At last!"

What's significant about the fact that God Himself "breathed the breath of life" into the man (v. 7)?

How was that different from God's relationship with the rest of creation?

What did the man's work in the garden say about the role of work in our lives (see vv. 8, 15).

What does God's statement "It is not good for the man to be alone" (v. 18) say about us as human beings?

How is this statement relevant for people who aren't married?

What's beautiful about the creation of marriage in verses 22-25?

Choose one of the previous questions and thank God
for the aspect of your life that it addresses.

DAY 3 • *GENESIS 3*

With Genesis 3 we now come to a crisis. Almost all great stories have
a crisis, because dealing with crises is a fundamental aspect of life. But
this crisis is the foundational crisis of human existence. As you read, think
about the different roles presented here.

What was each person doing and why?

The chapter tells us very important things about God and
about us as human beings. What was God's role in the
chapter, and what does the chapter tell us about God?

What do verses 1-6 tell us about temptation?

What do verses 7-24 tell us about the consequences
of sin?

Where is grace seen very clearly in this chapter?

How can this chapter help you deal with temptation
this week?

In what ways do you need God's grace in our fallen world
at this point in your life?

DAY 4 • REVELATION 19:6–20:6

Revelation 19:6–20:6 echoes our reading of Genesis 1–3 in profound ways. A few of points about Revelation:

1. It's a form of literature that generously uses symbols to speak of real relationships and dynamics.

2. The passage before us specifically deals with events at the end of the world, although that can't be said about all of Revelation.

3. Revelation embodies the gospel in a unique way to give strong encouragement to believers.

How does Revelation 19:6-10 echo specific parts of Genesis 1–3?

What does Revelation 19:6-10 tell us about the relationship God wants to have with us?

Revelation 19:11-21 depicts Christ judging evil in the world. What are the parallels here with Genesis 3?

What's the significance of the descriptors *priests* and *reign* in Revelation 20:6?

How do those descriptors echo Genesis 1–2?

What forms of injustice in the world do you long for God to put right?

How can Revelation 20:4-6 encourage the church today?

How does Revelation 20:4-6 encourage you?

A video interview that will help you understand the Book of Revelation can be found at *LifeWay.com/HeartofGodsStory*.

DAY 5 • *REVELATION 20:7–21:8*

As you read the passage for today, you may find images you don't fully understand, and that's OK. But there's much here that powerfully encourages us as we live for Christ today. Begin by looking for echoes of Genesis 1–3.

Take your time as you read, marking all the echoes of the first three chapters of the Bible. Then note all the references to death and life that run through the passage.

What part of the Revelation passage is sobering for you? Why?

What parts are especially beautiful promises that give you great encouragement?

What part of the passage would you like to learn more about?

DAY 6 • *REVELATION 21:9–22:21*

Today's reading brings us to the conclusion of the whole Bible. Again, notice the parallels with Genesis 1–3.

> How do the angels in Revelation 21:12, who are at the gates of the new Jerusalem, contrast with the cherubim of Genesis 3:24?

The images used throughout the Revelation passage speak of great glory to God (see 21:10-11). Interestingly, the shape of the city will be a cube, which is very hard to imagine, but this was also the shape of the holy of holies in the tabernacle in the Old Testament. So the city will be the ultimate place where people will live in God's presence forever. That's why there won't be a sanctuary in the new Jerusalem (see 21:22); the whole city will be a place where God will dwell and where people will worship Him. Today focus especially on 22:1-5.

> For what aspect of your life do you need hope at present?

> What needs healing in your life?

> How does the promise that Christ followers will see God's face (see 22:4) encourage you?

SCRIPTURE MEMORY

HIDING HIS WORD IN YOUR HEART

> He will wipe away every tear from their eyes.
> Death will no longer exist;
> grief, crying, and pain will exist no longer,
> because the previous things have passed away.
> REVELATION 21:4

GOING DEEPER

DEPTHS OF THE HEART
Revelation 21:3-7

This section will lead you step-by-step through an inductive study of the passage, using tools such as a study Bible, a Bible dictionary, and word-study helps. A template for Bible study can be found at LifeWay.com/HeartofGodStory.

> You're encouraged to watch the interview
> at LifeWay.com/HeartofGodsStory on how to interpret
> Revelation before you complete the following Bible study.

1. Gather your tools, beginning with a good study Bible and a Bible dictionary. If you have access to a good commentary on Revelation, get it as well. Suggestions for good commentaries are listed in step 6.

2. Thoughtfully read the passage in at least three different translations, noting any differences in the translations.

What strikes you about the passage?

3. What's the broader literary context of the passage? Begin by asking how the passage relates to Revelation 19–22.

Remember, with literary context we're trying to understand how this passage fits and functions in the book. As noted last week, one way to discern the broader context of a Scripture passage is to look at an outline of the whole book, which you can find in your study Bible or Bible dictionary. So look up Revelation in one of those tools and write your insights here.

Where does this passage fit? How does it seem to function in the book?

What would you say is the main theme of this passage? Why?

4. Read Revelation 21:3-7 again very closely, answering the following questions.

Who are the main actors in the passage (the people who are referred to)?

What are the contrasts in the passage?

What are the main actions in the passage? Are there any cause-and-effect dynamics?

Can you identify the two main movements in the passage?

What marks the beginning of the second movement?

5. Do word studies of the terms *faithful* and *true* in verse 5.

An overview of how to do word studies can be found at *LifeWay.com/HeartofGodsStory.*

What's the range of possible meanings for each Greek word?

Faithful:

True:

Identify three to five other passages for each term in which this same Greek word is used in a similar way.

Faithful:

True:

Based on the context of the passage, what do you think are the best translations of the words as they're used in this passage?

6. Read the notes in your study Bible.

If you also have access to commentaries, use them now. Here are a few commentaries to consider for further study:

Beale, G. K. *The Book of Revelation. The New International Greek Testament Commentary.* Grand Rapids, MI: Eerdmans, 2013. (Advanced)

Keener, Craig S. *Revelation. The NIV Application Commentary.* Grand Rapids, MI: Zondervan, 2009.

Mounce, Robert H. *The Book of Revelation. The New International Commentary on the New Testament.* Grand Rapids, MI: Eerdmans, 1997.

Osborne, Grant R. Revelation. *Baker Exegetical Commentary on the New Testament.* Ada, MI: Baker, 2002. (Advanced)

What are your key insights into the passage?

7. How does this passage touch on broader theological themes in the Bible? Provide examples of cross-references to other Scripture passages.

An overview of how to study the broader theological context in the Bible can be found at *LifeWay.com/HeartofGodsStory*.

Theme 1:

Theme 2:

Theme 3:

8. Apply the passage.

What would the passage have meant to the original readers of Revelation? What was the main point for them?

In what ways are we similar to the original audience? How are we different?

To what various aspects of our lives might the truth of this passage apply?

What's a specific application for your life?

JOURNALING

EXPRESSIONS OF THE HEART

Knowing God's Face

START

SHARING YOUR HEART

Start the session by sharing what group members learned or truths that were especially meaningful during last week's personal study. If needed, use the following review questions.

1. What's one main point that arrested your attention in week 2? How could that insight make a difference in your life?

2. What does Genesis 1 tell us about God? About us as human beings? Why is Genesis 1 foundational for the big picture of the Bible?

3. How did reading the story in Genesis 2, about the creation of man and woman, stimulate your thinking about what it means to be human?

4. What in Genesis 3 might give us insight into our own experiences of temptation? Where do you see expressions of God's grace in Genesis 3?

5. How does Revelation 20:7–21:8 reflect main themes in Genesis 1–3? How does it point to the gospel?

6. What excites you about Revelation 21:9–22:21? The passage doesn't tell us everything we'll experience in the new heaven and earth; it merely gives hints. What seems to be the emphasis here? How does that encourage believers who struggle in following Christ?

Study with your group.

- Pray before watching video session 3.
- As you watch, complete the viewer guide on the next page.
- Following the video, use the discussion questions provided to finish your time together as a group.
- Encourage everyone to complete the personal study for week 3 before the next group session.

WATCH

HEARING GOD'S HEART

Are you passionate about _____ Christ, or are you satisfied with knowing about Him?

What Does It Mean to Know God's Face?

1. God desires a personal _____ with us.

   Covenant: A meaningful _____ between God and people

2. God desires a relationship of _____.

   The most foundational sin is to think that we know _____ than God.

   Biblical faith is not a leap into the _____. It is a step into the _____.

   Biblical faith: My _____ in God that what He has revealed in the world as true is something that I can step out on and depend on

3. God's presence and God's _____ always go together.

   In His Word God teaches us the right way to _____.

   God takes sin very seriously because He knows the _____ of sin and its _____ in our lives and in our relationship with Him.

4. God's presence is ultimately seen in the face of _____ _____.

Jesus' going to the cross was _____.

The crucifixion was _____.

Jesus' sacrifice on the cross deals with the problem of _____ so that we can be brought back before the face of God.

PERSONAL NOTES

....
....
....
....
....
....
....
....
....
....
....
....

Video sessions available for purchase at *LifeWay.com/HeartofGodsStory*
or for streaming with a subscription to *smallgroup.com*

DISCUSS

RESPONDING TO GOD'S HEART

1. What part of the video had the biggest impact on you? Why?

2. If we can't literally see God's face, why does the Bible use the term "God's face" to speak of knowing God's presence in our lives? What does this word picture communicate?

3. How do you respond to Dr. Guthrie's treatment of faith as trust? Can you give an example of this kind of faith? What difference does it make in the Christian life?

4. What happens when we focus attention on God's presence while ignoring His principles? What happens when we focus attention on God's principles while ignoring His presence?

5. What's your understanding of our mission and identity as Christians? The mission and identity of your church? What role does God's presence play in that mission and identity?

MEETING GOD IN THE STORY

RHYTHMS OF THE HEART

DAY 1 • *GENESIS 15; 17:1-8*

The account of God's reaching out to Abraham to establish a relationship with him is another foundational story in the Bible. In Genesis 12:1-3, when Abraham was 75 years of age, God promised to make him into a great nation. In Genesis 15 the patriarch was perhaps a decade older, and he was 99 years of age when Genesis 17 begins. Notice how Abraham's relationship with the Lord developed.

What are the main points in these passages?

What did God want Abraham to do?

What do these passages tell us about a relationship with God?

With what are you having to trust God at this point in your life?

How would you describe the state of your relationship with God?

DAY 2 • *EXODUS 33*

Exodus 32–34 comes at a critical point in the Book of Exodus, right in the middle of an extensive section on the building of the tabernacle. Exodus 32 records the event that precipitated the crisis. Exodus 34 shows that the crisis had been averted, because Moses again went up on the mountain and met with God.

What was the crisis?

In Exodus 32 Moses came down off the mountain of God to find the Israelites in open rebellion. God's judgment was that He would send the people up to the land of promise led by an angel, but God wouldn't go with them (see 33:1-3). This was the crisis.

How does 33:4-11 demonstrate why this was bad news for God's people?

What was Moses' response in the remainder of chapter 33?

Moses demonstrated an urgency or a desperation to know the presence of God. Why did he say that's important?

In what ways is your life as a follower of God distinct from people who don't know the Lord?

What would it look like for you to seek God's face and God's ways?

How do you think that's done today?

DAY 3 • *PSALMS 15; 24*

Meditate on these psalms, both of which speak very directly to our point this week that God's presence and God's principles always go together; These psalms don't propose sinless perfection in terms of behavior. Rather, they describe patterns that characterize a godly person who is walking with the Lord.

What patterns do you notice in these psalms?

The list in chapter 15 suggests that the way we treat other people really matters in our relationship with God. How is Psalm 24 a bit different?

What patterns in the way you treat other people could be improved?

In what ways do you need God's grace in our fallen world at this point in your life?

What might it mean to receive "righteousness from the God of [your] salvation" (24:5)?

Psalm 24:7-10 is a poetic way of welcoming God into your life, in effect saying, "God, I am opening the doors of my life to You." Welcome and worship Him today in prayer.

DAY 4 • HOSEA 2:14-23; 6:1-3

At times the prophets dramatically acted out a message from God. The prophet Hosea, who ministered during the eighth century B.C., lived out a message from God in a unique way: he married a prostitute. The prophet's marriage was a picture of God's relationship with the people of Israel. He loved them and agonized over their lack of faithfulness to Him. In Hosea 2:14-23 God spoke as a lover wooing His people back to Him. Notice the very descriptive language.

> What characterizes the grace of God in Hosea 2:14-23?

> How would you describe the kind of love God has for His people and what He wants in a relationship with people?

Hosea 6:1-3 describes repentance by which a person recommits to a relationship with God.

> As you think about your relationship with God, in what ways does it parallel the descriptions of Hosea 2:14-23?

> Would you describe your current relationship with God as thriving, distant, or somewhere in between? What would it look like for you to "strive to know the LORD" (6:3)?

> A video interview on how to understand the prophets in the Old Testament can be found at *LifeWay.com/HeartofGodsStory*.

DAY 5 • JOHN 1:1-18

Today's passage brilliantly and beautifully speaks to us of the incarnation (coming in the flesh) of Jesus, the Son of God. This passage is clear that Jesus, referred to as "the Word" in verse 1, was the Creator of the universe. Yet one of the most astounding claims of the Christian faith is that the Creator of the universe came to earth as a baby born in Bethlehem, Israel, to be face-to-face with us so that we could know Him. He became human to come be with us, to explain God the Father to us, and to die for us.

What do you learn about Jesus from this passage? Specifically, what does the passage say Jesus has done or does?

What parts of the passage speak about God's desire for us to know Him?

As you think about Jesus today, choose two ways John described the Word. Worship Him through these descriptions. For instance, you might thank Him for His life, light, creativity, or "grace and truth" (v. 14). Which ministry of Jesus do you need most today?

DAY 6 • *PHILIPPIANS 3*

In Philippians Paul wrote to the church in Philippi, in part to encourage believers to stand together in unity for the gospel of Christ. In Philippians 2 the apostle used Christ Himself as an example of emptying self for others. At the end of the same chapter, Paul pointed to Timothy and Epaphroditus as stellar Christian leaders who had poured themselves out in ministry. In Philippians 3 Paul offered himself as an example to be followed. His life focused on one thing: knowing Christ. He contrasted a life based on human abilities and religion (see vv. 2-6) with a life that's completely dependent on Christ and the righteousness that comes through faith in Him.

What are the other contrasts in the chapter?

What's involved in knowing Christ, according to the apostle's words here?

Are there things that get in the way of growing in your relationship with Christ? Talk to Him about those things today. Can you say with Paul, "My goal is to know Him" (v. 10)?

SCRIPTURE MEMORY

HIDING HIS WORD IN YOUR HEART

Let us strive to know the LORD.
His appearance is as sure as the dawn.
He will come to us like the rain,
like the spring showers that water the land.
HOSEA 6:3

GOING DEEPER

DEPTHS OF THE HEART
Exodus 33:11-17

This section will lead you step-by-step through an inductive study of the passage, using tools such as a study Bible, a Bible dictionary, and word-study helps. A template for Bible study can be found at *LifeWay.com/HeartofGodsStory*.

1. **Gather your tools, beginning with a good study Bible and a Bible dictionary. If you have access to a commentary on Exodus, get it as well.**

2. **Thoughtfully read the passage in at least three different translations, noting any differences in the translations.**

    What strikes you about the passage?

3. What's the broader literary context of the passage in relation to the entire book of Exodus?

Remember, with literary context we're trying to understand how this passage fits and functions in the book. As noted before, one way to discern the broader context of a Scripture passage is to look at an outline of the whole book, which you can find in your study Bible or Bible dictionary. Look up Exodus in one of those tools and write your insights here.

Where does this passage fit? How does it seem to function in the book?

What would you say is the main theme of this passage? Why?

4. Read Exodus 33:11-17 again very closely, answering the following questions.

Who are the main actors in the passage (the people who are referred to)?

The passage records a dialogue between Moses and God. How would you describe the dialogue?

What are the main actions in the passage? Are there any cause-and-effect dynamics?

How would you outline the passage?

5. Do word studies of the terms *favor* in verses 12-17 and *ways* in verse 13.

An overview of how to do word studies can be found at *LifeWay.com/HeartofGodsStory*.

Favor:

Ways:

What's the range of possible meanings for each Hebrew word?

Favor:

Ways:

Identify three to five other passages for each term in which this same Hebrew word is used in a similar way:

Based on the context of the passage, what do you think are the best translations of the words as they're used in this passage?

6. Read the notes in your study Bible.

If you also have access to commentaries, use them now. Here are a few commentaries to consider for further study:

Bruckner, James K. *Exodus, Understanding the Bible Commentary Series.* Grand Rapids, MI: Baker, 2008.
Ross, Allen, John N. Oswalt, and Philip W. Comfort. *Genesis, Exodus, Cornerstone Biblical Commentary.* Carol Stream IL: Tyndale, 2008.
Stuart, Douglas K. *The New American Commentary.* Vol. 2, *Exodus.* B&H, 2006.

What are your key insights into the passage?

7. How does this passage touch on broader theological themes in the Bible? Provide examples of cross-references to other Scripture passages.

Theme 1:

Theme 2:

An overview of how to study the broader theological context in the Bible can be found at *LifeWay.com/HeartofGodsStory*.

8. Apply the passage.

What would the passage have meant to the original readers of Exodus? What was the main point for them?

In what ways are we similar to the original audience? How are we different?

To what various aspects of our lives might the truth of this passage apply?

What's a specific application for your life?

JOURNALING

EXPRESSIONS OF THE HEART

Thriving in God's Space, Part 1: The Tabernacle and the Temple in the Old Testament

START

SHARING YOUR HEART

Start the session by sharing what group members learned or truths that were especially meaningful during last week's personal study. If needed, use the following review questions.

1. What thoughts or questions have you had about God's presence in our lives since watching the previous session's video?

2. Which Old Testament passage from the readings this week (days 1–4) was your favorite and why?

3. Share one insight into God's presence in our lives that you gained from your personal study this week.

4. Where in the readings this week did you see the weaving together of God's presence and God's principles? How do God's guidelines for living integrate with a life of faith (trust)?

5. John 1:1-18 describes God as coming to meet us face-to-face in the person of His Son, Jesus Christ. How is this manifestation of God's presence different from descriptions of God's presence in the Old Testament passages? How does it build on those passages about God's presence?

Study with your group.

- Pray before watching video session 4.
- As you watch, complete the viewer guide on the next page.
- Following the video, use the discussion questions provided to finish your time together as a group.
- Encourage everyone to complete the personal study for week 4 before the next group session.

WATCH

HEARING GOD'S HEART
The Tabernacle: A Mobile Home for God

Description of the Tabernacle

Cherubim: Spiritual beings especially associated with the throne and the _____ of God

The tabernacle was in the _____ of the camp.

God's _____ was at the center of God's presence.

Functions of the Tabernacle

1. The tabernacle was a place of mediated relationship through _____.

    Atonement—the cleansing of sin through _____— was at the center of the function of the tabernacle.

2. The tabernacle is a place of rhythmic _____ at the center of the camp.

3. The tabernacle is a place of God's active presence for the manifestation of God's _____.

The Temple: Solomon's Big Project

Attention to the _____ of God is always related to the _____ of God.

Differences Between the Temple and the Tabernacle

1. Solomon is more like _____ than Moses.

2. God does not _____ the building.

3. The people do not freely _____ in the building.

4. The craftsmen are not _____ selected and empowered by God.

What We Learn from Solomon's Story

1. God's amazing _____ in working with flawed people and flawed projects

2. _____ for something better

PERSONAL NOTES

....

....

....

Video sessions available for purchase at *LifeWay.com/HeartofGodsStory* or for streaming with a subscription to *smallgroup.com*

DISCUSS

RESPONDING TO GOD'S HEART

1. What did you learn about the tabernacle in this session? What surprised you?

2. Without looking at your notes, can you recall the three functions of the tabernacle? How do those functions parallel our experience of church today?

3. What does the structure of the tabernacle tell us about God?

4. What did you learn about Solomon's temple?

5. In what ways do Solomon's compromises provide a cautionary tale for the people of God in our culture today? What are some expressions of God's grace in the story?

6. How does Solomon's story provide a framework for understanding the trajectory of the rest of the Old Testament story?

7. What's one practical lesson that you can take away from this session to apply to your life?

MEETING GOD IN THE STORY

RHYTHMS OF THE HEART

DAY 1 • *EXODUS 35–36*

Notice the context of the passage today. In Exodus 24 God and the people of Israel entered a covenant relationship. In Exodus 25–31 God gave instructions about building the tabernacle. In Exodus 32 the people sinned with the golden calf, and in Exodus 33–34 the covenant relationship with Yahweh was restored through Moses as the mediator. Now in Exodus 35 the people began to build the tabernacle. The illustrations on pages 138–39 will help you visualize the tabernacle and its components as you study them.

Why do you think Moses began in verses 1-3 by reviewing the Sabbath command?

In what ways did the people participate in the building, according to Exodus 35:4–36:7?

Carefully read the remainder of chapter 36 and list the parts of the tabernacle as you visualize them.

In what ways does this part of the story offer us an example of a community that works together for God's agenda in the world?

How can you generously contribute to the work of God this week?

DAY 2 • *EXODUS 37–38*

Exodus 37–38 focuses on the construction of the furnishings to be placed in the tabernacle. These furnishings would play a part in the daily sacrifices of the priests, and the altar of incense and the ark behind the veil would play special roles on the Day of Atonement (see Lev. 16), the one time a year when the high priest would make a sacrifice to cover all the sins that weren't already covered by other sacrifices.

The table described in Exodus 37:10-16 held the bread of the presence, which in part represented fellowship with God. Why do you think bread was used?

The lampstand gave light inside the tent and was shaped like a tree. Where else did important trees or bushes on fire come in the story of the Old Testament or in Exodus specifically?

What do you notice in the remainder of the passage today that seems to be a significant pattern in the organization of the tabernacle?

What can we learn about worship from this section of Scripture?

Is there structure to your worship of God? Why or why not?

DAY 3 • *EXODUS 39–40*

First Peter 2 says followers of Christ are priests (see vv. 5,9). What can you learn about the backdrop of this concept from the passage today? Exodus 40 says the priests were consecrated to God's purposes by being washed with water and anointed.

Have believers in Christ experienced something similar?

What's significant about the way chapter 40 ends?

What do we learn from chapters 39–40 about the presence of God among His people?

What patterns do you see in the organization of the old-covenant worship system that form a backdrop for understanding the message of the New Testament?

How can this passage encourage or strengthen your worship of God today?

Take time to worship God now.

DAY 4 • *1 KINGS 3:1-15; 5:1-18*

In some ways 1 Kings 3:1-3 sets the tone for the whole Solomon narrative.

What clues do you see here that King Solomon was very much a person of mixed character right from the beginning?

In 1 Kings 5 how was the building of the temple different from the building of the tabernacle in Exodus? The illustrations on page 140 will help you visualize the temple and its components as you study them.

At first 1 Kings 3 and 5 sound like celebrations of Solomon and the building process, but be sure to read the clues the narrator crafted into the story to indicate that more was going on here.

Spiritually, all of us are "mixed bags" at times in our lives. Do you know of situations in which a sincere leader who talked about God a lot was shown to be flawed in character?

What aspects of Solomon's story are enlightening for your life?

What traits of Solomon are most similar to your character?

A video interview on reading Old Testament stories can be found at *LifeWay.com/HeartofGodsStory*.

DAY 5 • I KINGS 6–7

First Kings 6 describes the building of Solomon's temple.

How long did it take to build the temple?

Why were such specific details provided about the building of the temple?

What's the focus of 7:1-12? Why is the location of this passage, in the middle of the story on the temple, significant?

Compare the buildings in Solomon's palace complex to the temple. Also notice the resumption of the building of items related to the temple in 7:15. What strikes you about these items?

In what ways can we be tempted to put our projects in life before the building of the Lord's "temple," the people of God (see I Pet. 2:5)?

Take time to evaluate your priorities at this point in your life. How do they align with God's priorities for your life?

DAY 6 • *1 KINGS 8:1–9; 9; 11:1-13*

In some ways 1 Kings 8 is a high point in the Old Testament. Remember that the building of the temple was accomplished fairly early in Solomon's reign, so the context here is important. But the passages in chapters 9 and 11 fill out the story, providing us with additional information. Notice that God qualified His blessing of the temple and Solomon's reign on several occasions. This wasn't an accident. In some ways it prepares us for the disastrous ending of the story. Later, in 9:10-14, some of the land of Israel was given back to a Canaanite, who then had buyer's remorse.

How do you respond to the end of the story in 11:1-13?

Was this a sudden development, or have we seen clues all along that this was coming?

Patterns of unfaithfulness are just that—patterns. Are you aware of any tendencies in your life that could develop into patterns of unfaithfulness if not attended to? Reflect on this question today and talk to the Lord about it, crying out to Him for strength to turn away from sin.

SCRIPTURE MEMORY

HIDING HIS WORD IN YOUR HEART

LORD God of Israel,
there is no God like You
in heaven above or on earth below,
keeping the gracious covenant
with Your servants who walk before You
with a whole heart.
1 KINGS 8:23

GOING DEEPER

DEPTHS OF THE HEART
I Kings 8:56-61

This section will lead you step-by-step through an inductive study of the passage, using tools such as a study Bible, a Bible dictionary, and word-study helps. A template for Bible study can be found at *LifeWay.com/HeartofGodsStory*.

1. Gather your tools, beginning with a good study Bible and a Bible dictionary. If you have access to a good commentary on Exodus, get it as well.

2. Thoughtfully read the passage in at least three different translations, noting any differences in the translations.

What strikes you about the passage?

3. What's the broader literary context of the passage in relation to the entire book of I Kings?

Remember, with literary context we're trying to understand how this passage fits and functions in the book. As noted before, one way to discern the broader context of a Scripture passage is to look at an outline of the whole book, which you can find in your study Bible or Bible dictionary. So look up I Kings in one of those tools and write your insights here.

Where does this passage fit? How does it seem to function in the book? Give special attention to what happens in chapters 9–11.

What would you say is the main theme of this passage? Why?

4. **Read 1 Kings 8:56-61 again very closely, answering the following questions.**

This is a blessing. What's the context of the blessing? Who is listening?

The passage has a good bit of repetition. What's the nature of the repetition?

What are the main actions in the passage? Are there any cause-and-effect dynamics?

How would you outline the passage?

5. **Do a word study of the term *rest* in verse 56 and choose one or two other terms in the passage on which to do word studies.**

What's the range of possible meanings for each Hebrew word?

Rest:

Identify three to five other passages for the term in which this same Hebrew word is used in a similar way:

Rest:

Based on the context of the passage, what do you think are the best translations of the word as it's used in this passage?

An overview of how to do word studies
can be found at *LifeWay.com/HeartofGodsStory*.

6. Read the notes in your study Bible.

If you also have access to commentaries, use them now. Here are a few commentaries to consider for further study:

House, Paul R. *1, 2 Kings*. Vol. 8, *The New American Commentary*. Nashville: Holman, 1995.
Provan, Iain W. *1 & 2 Kings. Understanding the Bible Commentary Series*. Grand Rapids, MI: Baker, 1993.

What are your key insights into the passage?

7. How does this passage touch on broader theological themes in the Bible? Provide examples of cross-references to other Scripture passages.

Theme 1:

Theme 2:

Theme 3:

An overview of how to study the broader theological context in the Bible can be found at *LifeWay.com/HeartofGodsStory.*

8. Apply the passage.

What would the passage have meant to the original readers of 1 Kings? What was the main point for them?

In what ways are we similar to the original audience? How are we different?

To what various aspects of our lives today might the truth of this passage apply?

What's a specific application for your life?

JOURNALING

EXPRESSIONS OF THE HEART

Thriving in God's Space, Part 2: Jesus and the Temple in the New Testament

START

SHARING YOUR HEART

Start the session by sharing what group members learned or truths that were especially meaningful during last week's personal study. If needed, use the following review questions.

1. Over the past week you've read about the Old Testament tabernacle and Solomon's temple. What do these passages tell us about God? What do they tell us about the condition of human beings?

2. How can individual believers and whole congregations best work to build rhythmic worship into their lives? What are hindrances to patterns of authentic worship? What's the biggest hindrance that you face personally?

3. What did Dr. Guthrie mean by God's active presence, as distinguished from the fact that theologically, God is present everywhere? What are some signs that God is actively present among us?

4. How did you respond to Solomon's story as presented in the video and in the personal study this week?

5. The narrative of 1 Kings shows that Solomon put his own house at the center of his life. As you've thought about your life this week, what are you tempted to put at the center of your life, in place of the work and worship of God?

Study with your group.

- Pray before watching video session 5.
- As you watch, complete the viewer guide on the next page.
- Following the video, use the discussion questions provided to finish your time together as a group.
- Encourage everyone to complete the personal study for week 5 before the next group session.

WATCH

HEARING GOD'S HEART

In the Old Testament story the _____ can't answer the problem. The _____ can't answer the problem. _____ cannot answer the problem.

At this point in the story, the ark of the covenant is now _____.

The glory of the Lord never again fills the _____ called the temple in Jerusalem.

The Temple Jesus Knew: Herod's Temple

For Jews, Jerusalem was the _____ of the world.

The temple was the center of religion, economy, and _____ power.

Jesus and the Temple

In Jewish theology when Messiah came, He would put things right with the _____.

Jesus would have been heard during His time as a _____ who was trying to subvert Judaism and the Roman government.

God is anticipating the time in the future when the Gentiles would flow into the city as _____ of God.

With Jesus' death and resurrection, the temple as the center for worship in the world is _____.

The Church as God's New Mobile Home

God changes the location of the temple. He transfers the templeness to His _____.

We're not only the temple; we're also the _____ in the temple, who can go right into the presence of the living God.

Your church building is not the primary way that God extends His grace to the world. _____ are.

The temple of God—the people of God on earth—are going to come together with the _____ dwelling place of God, and we're going to be with God forever.

PERSONAL NOTES

....

....

....

....

....

....

....

Video sessions available for purchase at *LifeWay.com/HeartofGodsStory* or for streaming with a subscription to *smallgroup.com*

DISCUSS

RESPONDING TO GOD'S HEART

1. What did you learn that surprised you about the backdrop of the temple Jesus knew?

2. How do the two problems of opposition and self-interest, which made the rebuilding of the temple difficult after the exile, factor into our work as the church today?

3. What did you learn about King Herod that you didn't know before?

4. What were main points Dr. Guthrie made about the significance of the temple for Jews during the time of Jesus? How do these dynamics make the story of Jesus' interaction with the temple come alive?

5. Is there a contradiction between the fact that the temple Jesus knew was built by someone who was neither Jewish nor religious and Jesus' calling the temple "My Father's house" (Luke 2:49)? Why or why not?

6. Some Jewish writers in the first century expected the Messiah to come and put things right with the temple. What are various ways Jesus did that?

7. In what ways is the day of Pentecost in Acts 2 a picture of God's tabernacling with His people? How does that experience encourage us to live out a dynamic walk with God?

MEETING GOD IN THE STORY

RHYTHMS OF THE HEART

DAY 1 • HAGGAI 1:1–2:9

Because of the rebellion and idolatry of God's people, the temple of Solomon was destroyed by the Babylonians in 587 B.C., and many Jews were taken into exile in Babylon. Having defeated the Babylonians, the Persian king Cyrus issued an edict in 538 B.C. that allowed the Jewish people to return to the land. In their second year back in the land, the people laid the foundation for a new temple (see Ezra 3:8-10). Yet because of opposition, lack of resources, and the people's preoccupation with their homes, the building of the temple was put on hold for 16 years.

The prophets Haggai and Zechariah came on the scene to motivate people to complete the building of God's house.

> As you read the passage for today, notice the repetition of the word *house*. What two houses are referred to?

> The people were struggling with various emotions and distractions in the passage. What were those emotions and distractions?

What did God say would be the result when the people got their priorities right?

How does the situation in Haggai 1:1–2:9 parallel the challenges we face today as we try to live for God in the modern world?

How might "the word of the LORD" (1:1) motivate us to stay focused on right priorities in our lives?

DAY 2 • LUKE 2:21-52

Read today's passage slowly, thinking about what you're reading. Take time to visualize the events that are being described. Also notice the role of the temple in this section of Luke's Gospel. In 2:21-38 Joseph and Mary took Jesus to the temple complex to dedicate Him to the Lord and offer a sacrifice. The account in 2:41-52 is the only story we have from the years when Jesus was growing up in Nazareth. Jesus was found at the temple complex discussing Scripture with the teachers. Remember, the temple complex was a huge public space, and the porches surrounding the complex would have been used for many purposes, including, perhaps, "Bible-study classes." You'll find illustrations of Herod's temple on page 141.

What do you think is the significance of this story?

What role does the temple play in the story, and what does the story tell us about Jesus' attitude toward the temple?

How are the events in today's passage relevant for you?

The stories from Jesus' infancy show that Jesus came, in line with God's Word in the Old Testament, to fulfill God's salvation. The event from His boyhood stresses Jesus' connection to the temple, the Scriptures, and His sense of identity in relation to God the Father.

In what ways does this passage fulfill Malachi 3:1?

"See, I am going to send My messenger, and He will clear the way before Me. Then the Lord you seek will suddenly come to His temple, the Messenger of the covenant you desire—see, He is coming," says the LORD of Hosts.
Malachi 3:1

DAY 3 • JOHN 2:13-25

Unlike Matthew, Mark, and Luke, John placed Jesus' cleansing of the temple at the beginning of his Gospel, and there are at least two possible reasons. It may be that Jesus cleansed the temple more than once, once at the beginning and again at the end of His ministry. However, John might have placed this event at the beginning of his narrative for theological emphasis, to stress the significance of the event. Jews of Jesus' day expected the Messiah to come and straighten out the temple worship. John may have put this event up front as a key to understand what his Gospel is all about: Jesus was going to build a new temple through His death, a temple that would consist of His followers, not a physical building.

There's possibly a double meaning here. Jesus first spoke of His own body as a sanctuary (see v. 19), but His words can also be read as anticipating His body, the church, God's new temple.

How can we become too focused today on the physical building we call the church?

How can we lose focus on the worship of God, shifting our view to a marketplace mentality?

One focus of our passage is on Jesus' authority to set things right. Are you submitted to His authority today?

DAY 4 • *ISAIAH 56:3-8; JEREMIAH 7:1-11; MATTHEW 21:12-13*

Matthew also has an account of the cleansing of the temple. How does it differ from and complement the account from John yesterday? We get a better understanding of the passage in Matthew if we read the context of Jesus' allusions to the Old Testament. Take time to read carefully the passages from Isaiah and Jeremiah.

Isaiah spoke of a time when Gentiles would fill God's courts as worshipers. It may be that the sellers and money changers Jesus confronted were in the court of the Gentiles in the temple. Thus, Jesus' action in part may have been to prepare the temple for what God was about to do for the Gentiles, fulfilled in Acts when God brought them salvation.

Jeremiah, on the other hand, focused on corrupt leadership. Can you see why the religious leaders would have been upset with Jesus? Can you see why many scholars believe Jesus' action in the temple got Him killed, from a human perspective?

> Jesus confronted a corrupt temple of His day for us. Praise Him today for His confrontation of evil in its many forms in the world.

> Praise Jesus for dying, rising, and building a new kind of temple, one that knows God's presence and participates in God's mission in the world.

A video interview on how to understand the New Testament story literature can be found at *LifeWay.com/HeartofGodsStory*.

DAY 5 • 2 CORINTHIANS 6:14–7:1

In 2 Corinthians Paul was dealing with a difficult situation. At least a significant minority of people in the church had been enticed by false teachers and no longer seemed committed to Paul, his mission, or the true gospel. So Paul wrote to them in 2 Corinthians 1:12–7:4 about the nature of authentic Christian ministry. The passage for today recounts the climax of his plea with this difficult church.

The verses about the sanctuary or temple in 2 Corinthians 6:14–7:1 are from Leviticus 26:11-12. Notice the emphasis on God's dwelling with His people and walking around with them. God's face and God's space came together in the theology of God's people as God's temple in the New Testament.

> From 2 Corinthians 6:14–7:1, what do grasping and living
> this perspective offer us for living the Christian life well?

> Do you see yourself as the dwelling place of God?
> What areas of your life need to be cleansed today
> so that you aren't mixing God's temple with idols?

DAY 6 • 1 PETER 1:13–2:17

Notice that, like 2 Corinthians 6:14–7:1 yesterday, 1 Peter also uses the image of the church as a temple in the context of speaking about our need for holiness. The fear spoken of in both passages doesn't refer to terror but rather to deep reverence or respect for God.

How does the temple imagery in 1 Peter 2:4-10 contribute to Peter's exhortation for us to be holy? How does this image of the temple give rise to other related images in verses 9-10?

What are the implications for Christ's people in being both "a spiritual house" and "a holy priesthood" (v. 5)?

What are our "spiritual sacrifices" (v. 5)? Think about our praise and our fellowship that we offer to God.

Spend time today offering fellowship and praise to God. Thank Him for making you a priest who can know His presence. Commit yourself in a fresh way to holiness.

SCRIPTURE MEMORY

HIDING HIS WORD IN YOUR HEART

We are the sanctuary of the living God, as God said:
I will dwell among them
and walk among them,
and I will be their God,
and they will be My people.
2 CORINTHIANS 6:16

GOING DEEPER

DEPTHS OF THE HEART
1 Peter 2:1-5

This section will lead you step-by-step through an inductive study of the passage, using tools such as a study Bible, a Bible dictionary, and word-study helps. A template for Bible study can be found at *LifeWay.com/HeartofGodsStory*.

1. **Gather your tools, beginning with a good study Bible and a Bible dictionary. If you have access to a good commentary on 1 Peter, get it as well.**

2. **Thoughtfully read the passage in at least three different translations, noting any differences in the translations.**

What strikes you about the passage?

3. What's the broader literary context of the passage in relation to the entire book of 1 Peter?

What would you say is the main theme of this passage? Why?

Remember, with literary context we're trying to understand how this passage fits and functions in the book. As noted before, one way to discern the broader context of a Scripture passage is to look at an outline of the whole book, which you can find in your study Bible or Bible dictionary. So look up 1 Peter in one of those tools and write your insights here.

Where does this passage fit? How does it seem to function in the book? What's gained by Peter's use of temple imagery?

4. Read 1 Peter 2:1-5 again very closely, answering the following questions.

Whom was Peter addressing? (Hint: take a quick look at the beginning of the book.)

What's the other main image or word picture used in the passage? (Hint: look for the words *like* or *as.*) What's the intersection of the two word pictures?

Who are the main actors in the passage (the people who are referred to)?

How would you outline the passage?

5. Choose two or three words from the passage to study.

An overview of how to do word studies
can be found at *LifeWay.com/HeartofGodsStory*.

What's the range of possible meanings for each Greek word?

Identify three to five other passages for each term in which
this same Greek word is used in a similar way.

Based on the context of the passage, what do you think
are the best translations of the words as they're used
in this passage?

6. Read the notes in your study Bible.

If you also have access to commentaries, use them now.
Here are a few commentaries to consider for further study:

Davids, Peter, H. *The First Epistle of Peter. The New International Commentary on the New Testament.* Grand Rapids, MI: Eerdmans, 1990.
Jobes, Karen H. *1 Peter. Baker Exegetical Commentary on the New Testament.* Grand Rapids, MI: Baker, 2005.
McKnight, Scot. *1 Peter. The NIV Application Commentary.* Grand Rapids, MI: Zondervan, 1996.
Schreiner, Thomas R. *1, 2 Peter, Jude. The New American Commentary.* Nashville: Holman, 2003.

What are your key insights into the passage?

7. How does this passage touch on broader theological themes in the Bible? Provide examples of cross-references to other places in Scripture.

An overview of how to study the broader theological context in the Bible can be found at *LifeWay.com/HeartofGodsStory*.

Theme 1:

Theme 2:

8. Apply the passage.

What would the passage have meant to the original readers of 1 Peter? What was the main point for them?

In what ways are we similar to the original audience? How are we different?

To what various aspects of our lives today might the truth of this passage apply?

What's a specific application for your life?

JOURNALING

EXPRESSIONS OF THE HEART

Extending God's Grace in the World

START

SHARING YOUR HEART
Start the session by sharing what group members learned or truths that were especially meaningful during last week's personal study. If needed, use the following review questions.

1. Do you often think about the fact that God lives in you right now as a part of His temple? How can that awareness make a difference in your patterns of life?

2. From the accounts in John and Matthew, how have you grown this week in your understanding of Jesus' cleansing the temple? Why is it necessary to understand the backdrop of the Old Testament story to grasp the significance of Jesus' radical action?

3. Why is it vital to understand the cleansing of the temple as a key to the whole gospel story?

4. Paul's temple theology is summarized in 1 Corinthians 6:19-20. This is one of the clearest expressions in the New Testament of God's design for the church as His new temple. How does this image change the way we see our lives?

5. First Peter 2:4-10 presents a beautiful word picture that combines temple, sacrifices, and priests. Why did Peter use these images? What did he want believers to understand about our relationship with God?

Study with your group.

- Pray before watching video session 6.
- As you watch, complete the viewer guide on the next page.
- Following the video, use the discussion questions provided to finish your time together as a group.
- Encourage everyone to complete the personal study for week 6.
- Discuss whether your group will meet for the optional session.

WATCH

HEARING GOD'S HEART

Grace: God's trustworthy _____ and _____ extended to us as He gifts us with all the good things we need

Ways God's Grace Is Extended to Us in the Heart of God's Story

1. God's grace _____.

   ### Types of Creative Grace

   1. All people experience _____ grace.

   2. _____ grace

2. God's grace _____.

   God, in the grand story of Scripture, keeps coming after His enemies to _____ us.

   There is a _____ and a _____ to grace.

   God's going to extend His grace through the Jewish people to the _____.

3. God's grace_____ and _____.

   Grace comes in to _____ things and make things the way they are supposed to be.

God's authority and power and love are going to have
to address _____ situations in the world.

4. God's grace _____ and _____.

If you are a person who is a part of the new covenant, you are not
before God.

God wants to extend grace _____ us so that He then can extend
grace _____ us.

PERSONAL NOTES

....
....
....
....
....
....
....
....
....
....
....
....
....

Video sessions available for purchase at *LifeWay.com/HeartofGodsStory*
or for streaming with a subscription to *smallgroup.com*

DISCUSS

RESPONDING TO GOD'S HEART

1. How has this session expanded your understanding of grace?

2. What are expressions of God's kindness and trustworthiness in your life this past week?

3. Dr. Guthrie talked about two kinds of creative grace: common grace and new-creation grace. Explain the difference between the two. How does this distinction help us grasp God's kindness to all people while emphasizing the necessity of having a personal relationship with God through the gospel?

4. What are some ways we can be creative in extending grace to those around us?

5. What does it mean that there's a tenacity to God's grace? How have you experienced that tenacity?

6. To what degree was the disruption of grace a new thought for you? What are examples of God's disruptive grace in your life? How did you grow stronger through such experiences?

7. Dr. Guthrie shared a number of word pictures to describe what happens when we enter a new-covenant relationship with God through Christ, including *salvation*, *forgiveness*, and *adoption*. Which one of these images means the most to you and why?

8. Each of us needs to enter God's story, express thanks to God for His initiating a relationship with us, and extend grace to people in the world. What specific commitments are you making as a result of this Bible study? How can God's Word, as you've encountered it in this Bible study, change patterns of your life in meaningful ways?

MEETING GOD IN THE STORY

RHYTHMS OF THE HEART

DAY 1 • *PSALM 136*

Read and meditate on this psalm today. Notice the emphasis on giving thanks at the beginning and the end of the psalm. Use the psalm to give thanks to God for specific things expressed in the psalm.

What are the various expressions of God's loving grace in this passage?

Why do you think the psalmist placed an emphasis on God's love as eternal? How does that encourage us?

Given the definition of *grace* shared in the video, how is even God's judgment of evil an expression of His grace?

Now read the psalm again, aloud if possible, and turn it into a prayer to God, using the refrain "Your love is eternal."

Finally, record the primary way God has expressed creative grace to you lately.

DAY 2 • JEREMIAH 31:1-34

Jeremiah's ministry started in about 627 B.C., as the nation of Babylon was on the rise as a world power. God used Babylon to judge the rebellious nation of Judah, and much of the Book of Jeremiah speaks of God's judgment of His people. However, Jeremiah 30–33, the section in which today's passage is found, brings a message of hope.

> As you read Jeremiah 31:1-34, mark all the expressions of God's grace and all the ways that grace was to give hope to God's people. Pay special attention to 31:31-34, a prophecy about the new covenant, a new way God would relate to His people. What are the characteristics of the new-covenant person's relationship with God, as described in this passage?

The New Testament explains that this new covenant was brought about by Jesus' ministry, death, and resurrection (see, for example, Luke 22:20; Heb. 8:7-13; 10:11-22).

> Which expression of God's grace in Jeremiah 31 do you need most in your life at this time?

> Spend time thanking God for His amazing kindness in offering a covenant by which our sins are decisively forgiven.

DAY 3 • ACTS 14

In the video we saw that Acts 14 speaks of both God's common grace (His good gifts to all people) and God's new-creation grace (salvation proclaimed through a relationship with Jesus). Carefully read the passage and watch for the author's emphases in this part of the story.

What did the author, Luke, want us to see about the early Christian movement?

How did Paul begin with common grace and move to what he saw as even more significant?

Where do you see both disruptive and eruptive grace in the passage?

How do all these expressions of grace provide a holistic picture of God's work of grace in the world?

What are some aspects of God's common grace, seen in your cultural context, for which you can praise God? Think of a good and beautiful thing God has given people, even those who don't know Him.

What are some creative ways we can build on common grace to share new-creation grace with people?

How can you extend God's grace in your world today?

DAY 4 • *2 CORINTHIANS 1:1-11*

Paul often started his letters with "Grace and peace," a common Christian greeting in the first century. Today's passage specifically focuses on God as a God of comfort and encouragement in the face of human suffering for the gospel. Notice that Paul praised God in the midst of the difficult circumstances he had faced.

What are some ways Paul described various expressions of God's goodness and grace?

What was Paul's perspective on the way God particularly uses difficulties in life for good?

Aren't you glad God's grace is available in the most difficult situations of life? What challenges are you personally facing at present? No matter the cause of the difficulties, use this passage to praise God for His comfort and encouragement.

A video interview on how to understand the New Testament letters can be found at *LifeWay.com/HeartofGodsStory*.

DAY 5 • *ROMANS 5*

Paul wrote the Book of Romans from Corinth in about A.D. 56 or 57, desiring to give the church in Rome—a church he had yet to meet—a summary of his teaching about the gospel and the Christian life. Romans 5 stands as one of the most beautiful expressions of that gospel in all of Scripture.

Take time to read Romans 5 very carefully. Record the various ways God's grace is described in the passage.

Even if you don't understand all of what Paul discussed here, what parts stand out to you as especially powerful?

Which images seem the most striking?

What part of the passage gives you hope for your life at present?

Who is someone with whom you would like to share this passage?

Spend time praising God for the expressions of grace you see in this passage. If you haven't yet committed your life to Christ, do so now.

DAY 6 • *EPHESIANS 2*

Like Romans 5, Ephesians 2 offers an amazing description of what happens when God brings His salvation to us.

Carefully read the passage; you might consider doing so in two or three different translations.

Paul talked about *Gentiles,* a term that referred to anyone who wasn't Jewish. What did Paul say about those of us who are Gentiles?

Recall that at the temple in Jerusalem during Jesus' time, the court of the Gentiles was separated from the inner courts of the temple by a wall with placards that forbade Gentiles from going past that point. A Gentile who went farther would be killed on the spot. When Paul spoke of Christ's breaking down "the dividing wall of hostility" (v. 14), he was figuratively speaking of that wall in the temple. Paul was saying that by God's grace we've been included in God's people, with free, open access to the worship of God.

> Is the gospel message one of peace for you at this point? Why or why not?

> What do you need to do to live in God's grace more fully? Seek out a friend or a minister in the church to talk about fresh ways you can embrace God's grace and extend His grace to others in the world.

SCRIPTURE MEMORY

HIDING HIS WORD IN YOUR HEART

God, who is rich in mercy, because of His great love that He had for us, made us alive with the Messiah even though we were dead in trespasses. You are saved by grace!
EPHESIANS 2:4-5

GOING DEEPER

DEPTHS OF THE HEART
Ephesians 1:3-8

This section will lead you step-by-step through an inductive study of the passage, using tools such as a study Bible, a Bible dictionary, and word-study helps. A template for Bible study can be found at *LifeWay.com/HeartofGodsStory*.

1. **Gather your tools, beginning with a good study Bible and a Bible dictionary. If you have access to a good commentary on Ephesians, get it as well.**

2. **Thoughtfully read the passage in at least three different translations, noting any differences in the translations.**

   What strikes you about the passage?

3. **What's the broader literary context of the passage in relation to Ephesians?**

   Remember, with literary context we're trying to understand how this passage fits and functions in the book. As noted before, one way to discern the broader context of a Scripture passage is to look at an outline of the whole book, which you can find in your study Bible or Bible dictionary. So look up Ephesians in one of those tools and write your insights here.

Where does this passage fit? How does it seem to function in the book?

What would you say is the main theme of this passage? Why?

4. Read Ephesians 1:3-8 again very closely, answering the following questions.

What are all of God's positive actions in the passage?

What are the main terms that are repeated? How do these terms give focus to the passage?

What do you find beautiful in this passage?

What do you struggle to understand in this passage?

NOTE: The concepts of God's choosing and predestining us (see vv. 4-5) before the foundation of the world are topics of theological debate. Don't let that debate distract you from the beauty and power of what Paul was celebrating: various aspects of God's astounding grace. Whatever your theological understanding of these concepts, meditate on the wonder that in the gospel God has said, "I want you! I choose you for a relationship with Me, and I have planned for a long, long time how I was going to adopt you as My child through a relationship with Christ."

How would you outline the passage?

5. **Choose two or three words from the passage to study (for example, *blameless, favored,* or *lavished*).**

An overview of how to do word studies can be found at *LifeWay.com/HeartofGodsStory*.

What's the range of possible meanings for each Greek word?

Identify three to five other passages for each term, in which this same Greek word is used in a similar way.

Based on the context of the passage, what do you think are the best translations of the words as they're used in this passage?

6. Read the notes in your study Bible.

If you also have access to commentaries, use them now. Here are a few commentaries to consider for further study:

Arnold, Clinton E. *Ephesians. Exegetical Commentary on the New Testament.* Grand Rapids, MI: Zondervan, 2010.
O'Brien, Peter T. *The Letter to the Ephesians. The Pillar New Testament Commentary.* Grand Rapids, MI: Eerdmans, 1999.
Snodgrass, Klyne. *Ephesians. The NIV Application Commentary.* Grand Rapids, MI: Zondervan, 1996.
Thielman, Frank. *Ephesians. Baker Exegetical Commentary on the New Testament.* Grand Rapids, MI: Baker, 2010.

What are your key insights into the passage?

7. How does this passage touch on broader theological themes in the Bible? Provide examples of cross-references to other Scripture passages.

An overview of how to study the broader theological context in the Bible can be found at *LifeWay.com/HeartofGodsStory.*

Theme 1:

Theme 2:

8. Apply the passage.

What would the passage have meant to the original readers of Ephesians? What was the main point for them?

In what ways are we similar to the original audience?
How are we different?

To what various aspects of our lives today might the truth
of this passage apply?

What's a specific application for your life?

JOURNALING

EXPRESSIONS OF THE HEART

Optional Group Session

The Story Continues . . .

FINAL REVIEW

GETTING TO THE HEART OF IT ALL

Welcome everyone to your final session of *The Heart of God's Story*. Use the following questions to lead a time of review and reflection.

1. Which of the passages from the personal study this week spoke to you most deeply? Why?

2. How does the new-covenant passage Jeremiah 31:31-34 help us understand the gospel more fully? How can we use it to extend grace to others as we explain the good news to them?

3. Day 3 considered Acts 14 and the topic of common grace. What are examples of common grace, seen in people around you, for which you can praise God? Think of a good and beautiful thing God has given people, even those who don't know Him. How does common grace help us answer the question, How can sinful people sometimes do good and beautiful things?

4. How has your understanding of God's grace grown this week?

5. How has your understanding of the gospel grown throughout this Bible study?

6. What have been important insights into Scripture that will help you live for the Lord more faithfully and fruitfully?

7. How can we as individuals or as the church put the truths of this Bible study into practice in very tangible ways to extend God's grace, to thrive in God's space, and to know God's face?

8. What aspects of the story of Scripture are much more alive and clear to you after completing this Bible study?

JOURNALING

EXPRESSIONS OF THE HEART

APPENDIX

SELECTED ILLUSTRATIONS

THE TABERNACLE

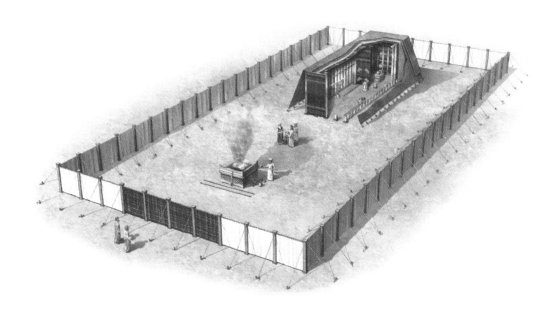

CUTAWAY OF THE TABERNACLE

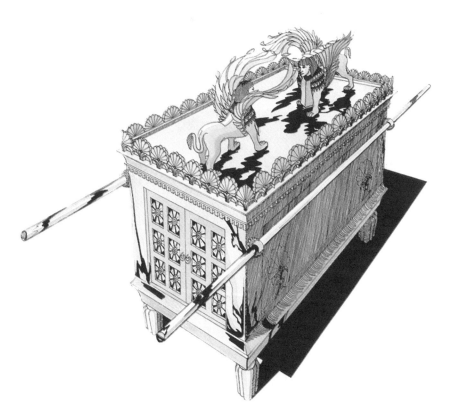

THE ARK OF THE COVENANT

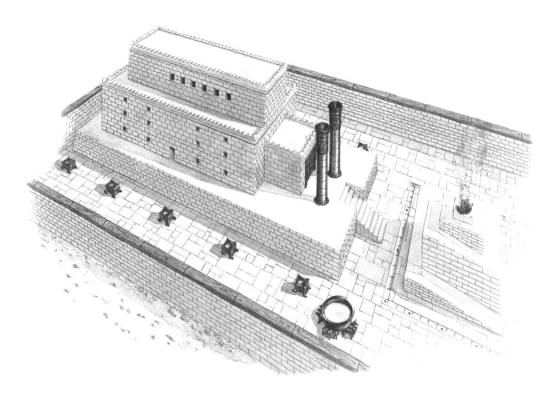

SOLOMON'S TEMPLE

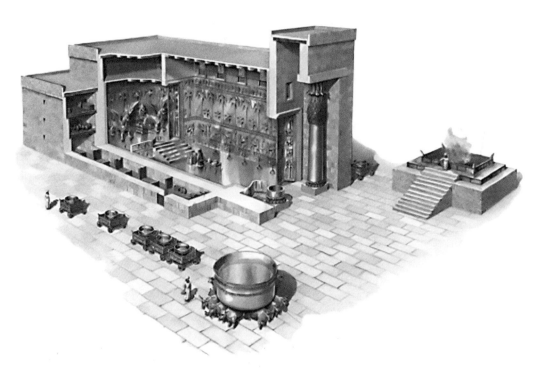

CUTAWAY OF SOLOMON'S TEMPLE

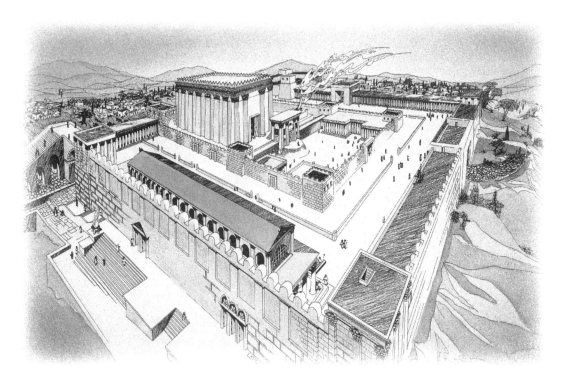

HEROD'S TEMPLE

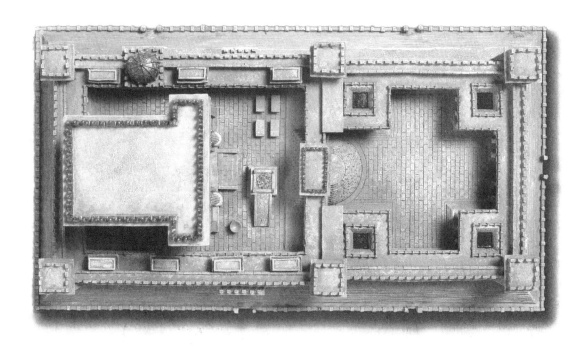

AERIAL VIEW OF HEROD'S TEMPLE

DVD

READ THE BIBLE FOR

LIFE

Listen. Understand. Respond.

GEORGE H. GUTHRIE

LifeWay
Biblical Solutions for Life

DO YOU UNDERSTAND THE BIBLE AS WELL AS YOU COULD?

God inspired the biblical writers to use a variety of literary types, including stories, poetry, proverbs, parables, and others. *Read the Bible for Life* teaches you how to read the various types of biblical literature in a way that unlocks God's intended meaning, enabling you to more accurately interpret the Bible and appropriately apply its teachings to your life. Once you understand the story of Scripture, you can better understand how you fit into that story.

READ THE BIBLE FOR **LIFE**

READER'S GUIDE TO THE BIBLE

Chronological Reading Plan

GEORGE H. GUTHRIE

foreword by DAVID PLATT

WANT TO READ THROUGH THE BIBLE IN ONE YEAR?

This chronological reading plan invites you into the world of the Bible and offers guidance for walking through its pages day by day. You'll see how the framework of the Bible's story can be laid out in 3 acts and 17 scenes. It even includes three foldout timelines to help you keep track of your place in the biblical story. This resource is designed to complement *Reading God's Story: A Chronological Daily Bible*, but it can be used as a companion to any Bible translation. Small-group discussion questions are provided at the end of each week for processing the week's readings with others.

WHERE TO GO FROM HERE

We hope you enjoyed *The Heart of God's Story*. If so, please share it on social media with #HeartofGod. Now that you've completed this study, here are a few possible directions you can go for your next one.

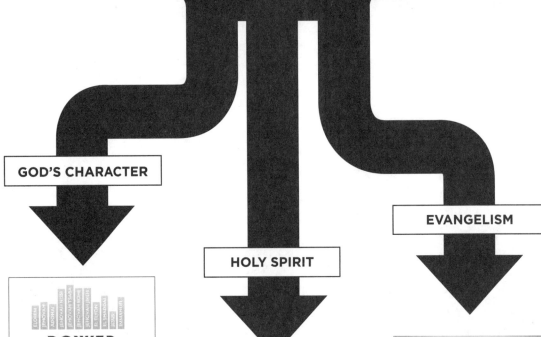

GOD'S CHARACTER

HOLY SPIRIT

EVANGELISM

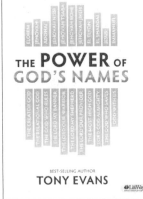

Learn the meanings of God's names to know Him more fully and experience Him more deeply. (6 sessions)

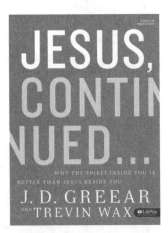

Go beyond the doctrines you already know to the Person Jesus wants you to know. (8 sessions)

Discover the simple joy of evangelism as the good news of Jesus naturally overflows into your daily life. (6 sessions)